THE UNBREAKABLE RULES

Logic, Integrity, and the Four Foundational
Pillars of Universal Ethics

"If you come seeking what you expect to find, this book will not offer it.

If you seek only confirmation, you will walk away with nothing.

But if you seek awareness, the beginning of seeing will unfold.

You choose whether to walk this path — or remain where you are."

Dedication

To all who hunger for

coherence in an age of noise.

May these pages steady your steps.

Acknowledgement

A book like this is never the work of one mind alone. It is the product of every conversation, every challenge, every moment of clarity and contradiction that has shaped my thinking over the years.

I want to acknowledge the people who sharpened my ideas not by agreeing with me, but by questioning me. Those who pushed back, who demanded coherence, who refused easy answers — you strengthened the very framework this book defends.

To the thinkers of the past — Heraclitus, Aristotle, Kant, Hume, Nietzsche — whose brilliance and boldness continue to illuminate the path of inquiry. Their disagreements are as valuable as their insights, for they reveal the terrain on which truth must be tested.

To the friends and readers who engaged with early drafts, who challenged assumptions, and who reminded me that clarity is an act of service. Your honesty and patience helped refine the arguments into something sharper, cleaner, and more accessible.

To those who believe that truth still matters — that coherence is not optional, that integrity is not outdated, and that rational discourse is still possible — this book is for you. Your courage to think clearly in a confused age is the reason these ideas needed to be written.

And finally, to every reader who opens this book with a willingness to examine their own mind: thank you. The pursuit of truth is a shared journey, and I am grateful to walk a part of it with you.

Preface

The Case for Unbreakable Rules

We live in an age where certainty is mocked, truth is optional, and morality is treated as a matter of taste. The loudest voices insist that ethics are nothing more than cultural habits or personal preferences — that no universal standard exists, and that every claim to truth is merely a disguised assertion of power.

Yet beneath the noise, something deeper remains.

Every human being — regardless of culture, education, or belief — relies on certain unspoken rules simply to think, speak, and act. These rules are not cultural. They are not political. They are not optional. They are the conditions for the possibility of rational life itself.

This book is an attempt to uncover those rules. It is not a manifesto.

It is not a religious treatise. It is not a political argument.

It is a philosophical excavation — a return to the bedrock beneath all disagreement.

We begin with the most fundamental principle of all: the Law of Non-Contradiction, the silent guardian of meaning. From there, we move to Intellectual Honesty, the discipline that keeps our minds aligned with reality. Finally, we build toward the Moral Ethics Baseline, the minimal set of universal moral rules that every functioning society must uphold.

These are not ideals. They are necessities.

This book is written for anyone who senses that the ground beneath our shared moral life is cracking — and who wants to rebuild that ground on something unbreakable.

If you are willing to think rigorously, question deeply, and confront uncomfortable truths, then this journey is for you.

Let us begin.

How To Read This Book

A Guide for Every Kind of Reader

This book is designed to be accessible to all readers —
whether you are a philosopher, a student, a leader, or simply
someone who wants to think more clearly.

1. Read Slowly, Not Passively

The ideas in this book are simple, but they are not shallow.
Pause often. Let the concepts settle. Challenge them.

2. Use the Examples as Anchors

Everyday analogies and illustrations are bridges, not
simplifications.

3. No Prior Philosophical Knowledge Needed

Aristotle, Kant, Hume, and Nietzsche appear only when
necessary — and always with clarity.

4. Pay Attention to the Four Pillars

Each pillar supports the next, forming a coherent structure:

Acknowledgment

LNC

Intellectual Honesty

Moral Ethics

5. Use the Book as a Mirror

This is not abstract ethics. It is about your thinking, your
integrity, your choices.

6. Expect Discomfort

Clarity, consistency, and courage are demanding virtues —
but liberating ones.

7. Keep the End in Mind

The goal is not to give you moral rules.
It is to give you the framework that makes moral rules
possible.

**Awakening is not the end of the journey.
It is the moment the real journey begins.**

In *The Burden of Comfort*, you confronted the first and most
necessary rupture:
the recognition that comfort is not safety, that ease is not
freedom, and that the self you inherited is not the self you
must become.

You saw the illusions that held you.
You felt the weight of the habits that shaped you.
You tasted the first breath of clarity.

But clarity is not transformation.
It is exposure.

When comfort falls away, the self stands uncovered — and
everything that was hidden beneath it rises to the surface.
This is where the thresholds appear.

Thresholds are not obstacles.
They are confrontations with the parts of yourself that resist
becoming.
They are the silent tests that reveal whether your awakening
was merely emotional…
or whether it can become structural.

The journey ahead is not about comfort or discomfort.
It is about coherence.

You will face thresholds of fear, thresholds of identity,
thresholds of truth, thresholds of integrity.
Each one demands something of you.
Each one asks whether you are willing to cross from who you
were into who you must become.

The first book awakened you.
This book will test you.

If you choose to continue, understand this:

Awakening opens the door.
Thresholds demand that you walk through it.

Let us begin.

Introduction

The Search for What Cannot Be Denied

Every ethical system in history — from Aristotle to Kant, from Confucius to Nietzsche — has attempted to answer the same question:

How should we live?

But before we can answer that question, we must confront a more fundamental one:

How do we know anything at all?

Ethics cannot float in midair. It must be anchored in something solid — something that does not change with fashion, culture, or personal preference.

This book argues that such a foundation exists, and that it is accessible to every rational mind. It is not mystical. It is not ideological. It is not culturally specific. It is the foundation you already use every time you think, speak, or make a decision.

We call these foundations **The Four Foundational Pillars**:

1. **Acknowledgment** — the conscious acceptance of reality as it is.

2. **The Law of Non-Contradiction** — the structure that makes meaning possible.

3. **Intellectual Honesty** — the discipline that aligns belief with evidence.

4. **Moral Ethics (Baseline)** — the universal moral floor required for human coexistence.

These pillars are not optional.
They are not invented.
They are discovered.

They are the rules you must adhere to simply to be a coherent agent in the world.

If you have ever felt that moral relativism leaves you unmoored, or that modern discourse has abandoned coherence, or that truth has become negotiable, then this book offers a way back to solid ground.

Not by appealing to authority.
Not by appealing to tradition.
But by appealing to logic, integrity, and the structure of reality itself.

Let us explore them together

Table of Contents

THE FOUNDATIONS OF RATIONAL AGENCY

Philosopher: Heraclitus

The Perpetual Challenge of Flux

Before we assert the stability of the Law of Non-Contradiction, we must confront one of the oldest and most profound challenges to the very idea of stable truth: the doctrine of Universal Flux, articulated by the pre-Socratic philosopher Heraclitus (c. 535–475 BCE).

Heraclitus famously declared:

"No man ever steps in the same river twice."

His point was not poetic but metaphysical: everything is always changing.

If everything is in constant motion, then nothing can be firmly defined.

If nothing can be defined, then nothing can be known. If nothing can be known, then no ethical rule can ever be universal.

This is the first great test of our framework.

The Challenge to Coherence

Heraclitus's doctrine directly attacks the starting premise of the Law of Non-Contradiction (LNC): that we can identify something as A "in the same respect and at the same time," as the classical formulation states.

If reality is pure flux, then:

A thing is never fully itself

A statement is never fully true

A rule is never fully binding

Under pure flux, coherence collapses

If nothing remains stable long enough to be identified, named, or understood, then the very conditions for thought dissolve. A world of pure becoming leaves no foothold for meaning.

But human beings do not — and cannot — live as if coherence collapses.
Our reasoning, language, and moral judgments all presuppose stability; without it, thought itself becomes impossible.

We make decisions.
We form intentions.
We act with purpose.
We distinguish between what is and what is not.

This reveals something crucial:

Even if the world changes, the mind must impose structure on that change to function at all.

This is where the LNC enters as the guardian of meaning.

The LNC's Response: The Necessity of Definition

The Law of Non-Contradiction does not deny change.
It denies *meaninglessness*.

To think, speak, or act, the agent must:

Identify something

Distinguish it from what it is not

Hold that distinction long enough to reason about it

This is the minimal requirement for consciousness.

Heraclitus shows us the river is always moving.
The LNC shows us that unless we can say "this is the river,"
we cannot step into it at all.

To stand in the river of reality, we must build the foundations that
make truth possible

Philosopher: Immanuel Kant

Universalization and Its Underlying Assumptions

Immanuel Kant (1724–1804) offered one of history's most
ambitious attempts to ground morality in reason through the
concept of Duty. His central principle, the Categorical
Imperative, urges us to act only on maxims we could will to
become universal laws. It is a noble rule, and on the surface it
appears rational and morally sound. Yet like every rule, it
quietly assumes a foundation. Kant never explains where the
evaluator's framework comes from — where the categories of
thought, the sense of reason, or the very standard of
universality originate. If these foundations rest on nothing
more than inherited habits of thought, then the rule stands on
sand, not stone.

This is not a criticism of Kant, but an invitation to awareness.
Before we trust any moral framework — whether ancient,
modern, or our own — we must ask a deeper question: What
is the reference point beneath my reasoning? If the ground is
unexamined, the structure built upon it will eventually crack.
Clarity begins when we recognize the source of our standards,
not merely the rules that arise from them.

But Kant begins with duty — with what one ought to do.
Our framework begins one step earlier:
with what is.

The Bridge to Coherence

To see this more clearly, we must look at the logical structure
that makes Kant's test possible.
Kant's universalization test relies on the Law of
Non-Contradiction.
When Kant asks whether a maxim can be universalized

without contradiction, he is invoking the LNC as the ultimate
judge of moral coherence.

Thus:
• Kant provides the moral test
• The LNC provides the logical machinery that makes the test
possible

Kant's ethics stand on the shoulders of the LNC.

Four Pillars Of Truth

Pillar 1 — Acknowledgment

The Foundational Axiom of Conscious Agency

Before logic, before ethics, before any rule or principle, there is a single voluntary act that makes rational life possible:

Acknowledgment.

Acknowledgment is the conscious acceptance of reality as it is — not as we wish it to be, not as we fear it to be, but as it presents itself.

It is the first "Yes" of the rational agent.

Without this initial act, nothing else can follow.

1. What "Law" Means in this Context

Acknowledgment is not a conclusion.
It is a beginning.

2. What Acknowledgment Implies

Acknowledgment carries three unavoidable implications:

A. Acceptance of the Facts

The agent must begin with what is, not with what they prefer.

B. Volitional Engagement

The agent must choose to participate in reality rather than retreat into denial.

C. Boundary Recognition

The agent must accept that reality has limits — and that those limits matter.

This is the antidote to escapism.

3. Implications for the Ethical Framework

A. Anti-Escapism

Acknowledgment forces the agent to use the actual facts as the input for ethical reasoning.

B. Precursor to the LNC

To test a proposition for contradiction, the agent must first acknowledge the components that define it.

Acknowledgment is the first step toward coherence.

Pillar 2 — The Law of Non-Contradiction

The Logical Test of Necessity

The Law of Non-Contradiction (LNC) is the firmest principle in classical logic.
It states:

A and not-A cannot both be true in the same respect and at the same time.

This is not a rule we invent.
It is a rule we discover — because without it, meaning collapses.

a. What "Law" Means Here

The LNC is an Axiom — a principle so fundamental that it cannot be proven by something more basic, because it is itself the basis of proof.

Its function is to be the boundary condition for meaning.

b. What the LNC Implies

The LNC implies:

Objective truth is non-negotiable

The world is structured

Argument is possible

Coherence is mandatory

Without the LNC, nothing can be affirmed or denied.

c. Implications for the Ethical Framework

A. Necessity

The LNC shifts ethics from preference to mandatory.

B. Integrity

The LNC demands consistency — the foundation of intellectual honesty.

Simple Illustrations

The Door

A door cannot be open and closed in the same respect at the same time.

The $100 Commitment

You cannot both keep and hand over the same $100 at the same moment.

Contradictions reveal impossibility.

The Hegelian Counterpoint

Hegel saw contradiction as the engine of development. But even in his dialectic, the goal is the resolution of contradiction in a higher unity.

Contradiction may drive growth —
but coherence remains the destination.

Here, "law" does not mean a statute or command.
It means a Primal Axiom of Agency — a foundational commitment that the agent must make in order to begin reasoning at all.

Philosopher: David Hume

The Challenge of Reasoning and the Is–Ought Divide

David Hume (1711–1776) is the philosopher who forces us to confront the limits of our own reasoning. His work is a mirror held up to the mind, exposing its habits, shortcuts, and illusions.

Hume's two great challenges are:

1. The Problem of Induction

We assume the future will resemble the past — but we cannot prove it.

2. The Is–Ought Problem

You cannot logically derive what ought to be from what is.

These challenges strike at the heart of any ethical system. If we cannot justify our reasoning, and we cannot move from facts to values, then how can we claim any moral rule is universal?

Hume forces us to confront a painful truth:

Reason alone cannot save us.

But Hume also gives us the key to the next step.

Pillar 3: Intellectual Honesty

The Scrutiny of the Framework

Hume demands radical self-awareness.
He exposes the mind's tendency to:

leap to conclusions

cling to habits

defend beliefs without evidence

confuse preference with truth

This is why Intellectual Honesty becomes necessary.

Hume's challenge is not a dead end.
It is a doorway.

He shows us that the mind is fallible

and therefore must be disciplined.

This discipline is Step 3 — Intellectual Honesty

The Protocol of Inquiry

Intellectual Honesty is the operational virtue of the rational agent.
It is the method by which we apply the LNC to our own thinking.

It demands:

truthfulness with oneself

resistance to bias

willingness to revise beliefs

commitment to evidence

courage to confront uncomfortable facts

If the LNC is the structure of coherence,

Intellectual Honesty is the practice of coherence.

What "Law" Means Here

This is not a logical axiom or a natural law.

It is a Volitional Law — a self-imposed internal directive.

It is the agent's promise to themselves:

"I am responsible for aligning myself with what is true."

2. What Intellectual Honesty Implies

A. Epistemic Humility

The willingness to admit when you are wrong.

B. Primacy of Evidence

Beliefs must be proportional to the evidence available.

C. Good Faith Engagement

Opposing views must be represented fairly, not caricatured.

Intellectual Honesty is the antidote to bias.

3. Implications for the Ethical Framework

A. Integrity in Action

Intellectual Honesty is how the agent becomes internally whole
when beliefs, values, and actions align.

B. Countering Cognitive Bias

Confirmation bias, motivated reasoning, and tribal loyalty collapse under honest scrutiny.

C. Trust in Discourse

Honest inquiry is the foundation of trust,
and trust is the foundation of any society.

Without Intellectual Honesty,
the LNC becomes a weapon rather than a guide.

Philosopher: Friedrich Nietzsche

The Challenge of Objective Value

Friedrich Nietzsche (1844–1900) is the most formidable critic
of universal morality.
He declared:

"God is dead."

By this he meant that the old foundations of value —
religion, tradition, metaphysics — had collapsed.

Nietzsche's two central challenges are:

1. Perspectivism

There are no moral facts — only interpretations.

2. The Will to Power

All human action is ultimately an expression of power.

If Nietzsche is right, then universal ethics is impossible.
Morality becomes a mask for domination.

This is the final and greatest test of our framework.

The Scrutiny of the Framework

Nietzsche demands:

Prove that your moral baseline is not arbitrary.

Our response is not theological.
It is not cultural.
It is not historical.

It is **logical**.

The LNC Constraint

A moral rule is universal if its universal negation leads to
contradiction.

The Intellectual Honesty Mandate

If you value your own agency,
you must — to remain coherent — value the agency of
others.

This is not sentiment.
It is necessity.

Thus, the Moral Ethics Baseline is not a preference.
It is a consequence of coherence.

Pillar 4 — Moral Ethics (Baseline)

The Coherent Content of Universal Morality

The Moral Ethics Baseline is not a minimal threshold.
It is not the lowest bar a society must clear.
It is the **absolute requirement** for any coherent and
functional human society.

This baseline represents the **highest non-negotiable ideal,**
the structural core without which moral order collapses into
contradiction.
It is the **rock-solid foundation** upon which all higher ethical
reasoning must stand.

These laws are **prescriptive because they are necessary**.
They arise not from culture, preference, or tradition,
but from the **logical structure of moral existence itself**.
To deny them is to deny coherence.

They are the **axioms of human coexistence —**
principles that cannot be violated without undermining the
very possibility of a stable society.

From their necessity follows a set of implications that shape
the moral landscape itself, revealing what coherence demands
of any being who seeks to live within it.

2. What the Baseline Implies

A. Necessity of Reciprocity

If you demand moral consideration for yourself,
you must — to remain coherent — extend it to others.

B. Universality of Suffering

Because all humans can suffer, arbitrary harm is universally
unjustifiable.

C. Inviolability of Agency

Agency is the foundation of rational life —
and therefore cannot be violated without contradiction.

3. Implications for the Ethical Framework

A. Defeating Moral Relativism

The Baseline is the answer to relativism.
It shows that some moral rules are universal because their
denial is incoherent.

B. Foundation for Moral Growth

The Baseline is not the end of ethics.
It is the beginning.

It provides the stable ground from which higher virtues can
grow.

Appendix A — Summary of the Four Foundational Pillars

This appendix provides a concise overview of the entire framework.

It is designed for quick reference, study, and practical application.

Pillar 1 — Acknowledgment

The Foundational Axiom of Conscious Agency

- The voluntary acceptance of reality as it is.

- The first act of rational engagement.

- The antidote to denial, distortion, and escapism.

- The necessary precursor to all logical and ethical reasoning.

Without acknowledgment, nothing else can begin.

Pillar 2 — The Law of Non-Contradiction (LNC)

The Logical Test of Necessity

- A and not-A cannot both be true in the same respect and at the same time.

- The boundary condition for meaning.

- The structure that makes truth, argument, and coherence possible.

- The logical foundation beneath all universal ethics.

Without the LNC, nothing can be true or false.

Pillar 3 — Intellectual Honesty

The Protocol of Inquiry

- The discipline of aligning belief with evidence.

- The practice of resisting bias and self-deception.

- The volitional commitment to truth over comfort.

- The operational form of integrity.

Without intellectual honesty, coherence collapses into

self-serving illusion.

Pillar 4 — Moral Ethics (Baseline)

The Coherent Content of Universal Morality

- The absolute, non-negotiable moral foundation
  required for any functioning society.

- Derived from logical necessity, not cultural
  preference.

- Grounded in reciprocity, agency, and the universality
  of suffering.

- The starting point for all higher moral development.

Without the baseline, society becomes incoherent and
self-destructive.

Appendix B — Everyday Applications of the Four Pillars

This appendix offers simple, practical examples of how the Four Pillars operate in daily life.

1. Conflict Resolution

- **Acknowledgment:** Recognize the actual issue, not the imagined one.
- **LNC:** Identify contradictions in claims or expectations.
- **Intellectual Honesty:** Admit your own contribution to the conflict.
- **Moral Ethics:** Treat the other person's agency as equal to your own.

2. Decision-Making

- **Acknowledgment:** Assess the real situation.
- **LNC:** Remove contradictory goals or assumptions.
- **Intellectual Honesty:** Evaluate evidence without bias.
- **Moral Ethics:** Choose the option that respects universalizable principles.

3. Public Discourse

- **Acknowledgment:** Begin with shared facts.
- **LNC:** Expose contradictions in arguments.
- **Intellectual Honesty:** Represent opposing views fairly.
- **Moral Ethics:** Avoid positions that violate agency or reciprocity.

GLOSSARY OF KEY TERMS

A clear, accessible glossary for readers of all backgrounds.

Acknowledgment

The conscious acceptance of reality as it is, without distortion or denial.

Agency

The capacity of a conscious being to make choices and act upon them.

Axiom

A foundational principle that cannot be proven by something more basic.

Baseline (Moral Ethics)

The minimal, non-negotiable moral rules required for any functioning society.

Coherence

Internal consistency within a belief system or argument.

Contradiction

A pair of statements that cannot both be true in the same respect and at the same time.

Epistemic Humility

The willingness to admit the limits of one's knowledge.

Intellectual Honesty

The discipline of aligning belief with evidence and resisting bias.

Integrity

The state of being internally whole — when beliefs, values, and actions align.

Law of Non-Contradiction (LNC)

The principle that contradictory propositions cannot both be true.

Natural Moral Law

Moral principles derived from the conditions of human existence and cooperation.

Necessity (Logical)

A truth that cannot be otherwise without collapsing coherence.

Perspective (Nietzschean)

A viewpoint shaped by individual drives and interpretations.

Universalization

Kant's test for whether a maxim can be applied universally without contradiction.

RECOMMENDED READING

These works deepen the themes explored in this book. They are not required, but they enrich the philosophical landscape.

Classical Logic & Foundations

- **Aristotle —** *Metaphysics*
  Especially Book IV on the Law of Non-Contradiction.

- **Thomas Aquinas —** *Summa Theologiae*
  Sections on truth, being, and natural law.

Modern Philosophy

- **Immanuel Kant —** *Groundwork of the Metaphysics of Morals*
  The foundation of universalizable ethics.

- **David Hume —** *An Enquiry Concerning Human Understanding*
  The problem of induction and the limits of reason.

- **Friedrich Nietzsche —** *Beyond Good and Evil*
  The critique of objective morality.

Contemporary Works on Reasoning

- **Daniel Kahneman —** *Thinking, Fast and Slow*
  Cognitive biases and the architecture of thought.

- **Jonathan Haidt —** *The Righteous Mind*
  Moral psychology and the roots of disagreement.

SUMMARY

The Unbreakable Rules: Logic, Integrity, and the Four
Foundational Steps of Universal Ethics

In a world drowning in opinions, contradictions, and moral
confusion, one question rises above the noise:
Is there anything we can all agree on — anything truly
universal?

This book answers with a bold yes.

The Unbreakable Rules reveals the hidden architecture
beneath all rational thought and ethical action.
It uncovers the Four Foundational Steps —
Acknowledgment, the Law of Non-Contradiction, Intellectual
Honesty, and the Moral Ethics Baseline — the principles
every human being must use simply to think, speak, or act
coherently.

These are not cultural values.
They are not political positions.
They are not subjective preferences.
They are logical necessities — the rules that make meaning
possible.

Through clear reasoning, vivid examples, and powerful
philosophical analysis, this book dismantles moral relativism,
exposes self-contradictory worldviews, and rebuilds ethics on
a foundation that cannot be shaken.

Whether you are a philosopher, a leader, a student, or
someone seeking clarity in a chaotic age, this book offers a
path back to solid ground —
a framework for thinking and living with coherence, integrity,
and purpose.

ABOUT THE AUTHOR

Conde D. Cagalitan is a philosopher and writer whose work explores the foundations of truth, the nature of awakening, and the inner transformation required for genuine human renewal. His thinking is rooted in classical realism and a deep conviction that truth is objective, unchanging, and the only reliable ground for a meaningful life.

Drawing from years of disciplined reflection, he writes to guide readers through the difficult but necessary journey of self-examination, humility, and rebirth of the heart. His books combine metaphysical clarity with poetic resonance, offering a path toward integrity in an age marked by confusion, fragmentation, and the loss of the sacred.

He lives in Australia, where he continues to develop a trilogy on awakening and renewal, alongside accessible works designed to help readers live truthfully in their daily lives.